Guts

Guts

Raina Telgemeier
with color by Braden Lamb

An Imprint of
SCHOLASTIC

All rights reserved. Published by Graphix, an imprint of Scholastic Inc.,
Publishers since 1920. SCHOLASTIC, GRAPHIX, and associated logos are trademarks
and/or registered trademarks of Scholastic Inc. All other trademarks are the
property of their respective owners and are used without permission.

The publisher does not have any control over and does not assume any
responsibility for author or third-party websites or their content.

This graphic novel is based on personal experiences, though certain
characters, places, and incidents have been modified in service
of the story.

Library of Congress Cataloging-in-Publication Data

Names: Telgemeier, Raina, author, illustrator.
Title: Guts / Raina Telgemeier ; with color by Braden Lamb.
Description: First edition. | New York, NY : Graphix logo, an imprint of Scholastic, 2019.
Identifiers: LCCN 2018050676 (print) | LCCN 2018060290 (ebook)
ISBN 978-0-545-85253-1 (ebook)
ISBN 978-0-545-85251-7 (hardcover : alk. paper)
ISBN 978-0-545-85250-0 (pbk. : alk. paper)
Subjects: LCSH: Stress in children. | Children-Physiology. | Stomach-Diseases.
Classification: LCC BF723.S75 (ebook) | LCC BF723.S75 T45 2019 (print) | DDC 155.4/189042-dc23
LC record available at https://lccn.loc.gov/2018050676

10 9 8 7 6 5 4 3 2 1   19 20 21 22 23
Printed in China   62
First edition, September 2019
Edited by Cassandra Pelham Fulton
Lettering by Jesse Post
Book design by Phil Falco
Author photo by Joseph Fanvu
Publisher: David Saylor

For anyone who feels afraid

1

2

TRY TO DO IT. YOU'LL FEEL BETTER.

. . .

I DON'T KNOW HOW.

WELL, WHEN YOUR BODY IS READY, YOU'LL JUST --

HRK!

4

HRMKFLP!!

BLEAHHHH

HONEY -- MOVE -- I NEED TO --

FOURTH GRADE WAS PRETTY MUCH ONE LONG GROSS-OUT CONTEST.

BRAP BRAP BRAP BRAP

ENCYCLO-PEDIA of GROSS THINGS!

COFFEE...

TEA...

MILK-SHAKE...

PEE!!

PTHBBLTTT!

HEY!

GUYS!!

THE STOMACH FLU MADE THE ROUNDS TO A LOT OF US THAT SEASON.

TEDDY SHANAHAN BARFED IN THE MIDDLE OF THE YARD AT THE END OF RECESS...

AND HE DROPPED HIS **PENCIL** IN IT!

POOR TEDDY.

I WOULD **NOT** WANT THAT TO HAPPEN TO ME.

A FEW DAYS LATER, WHEN TEDDY RETURNED TO SCHOOL . . .

PENCIL PUKE!!!

PENCIL PUKE!

PENCIL PUKE!

PENCIL PUKE!

Ha Ha Ha

PENCIL PUKE!

Ha Ha Ha

Ha Ha

Chew

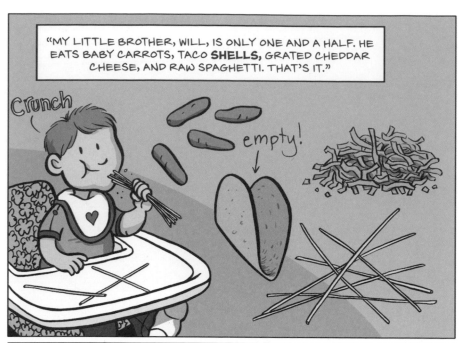

"MY LITTLE BROTHER, WILL, IS ONLY ONE AND A HALF. HE EATS BABY CARROTS, TACO **SHELLS**, GRATED CHEDDAR CHEESE, AND RAW SPAGHETTI. THAT'S IT."

Crunch

empty!

"MY SISTER, AMARA, IS FIVE. SHE LIKES SALAD. AND FRENCH FRIES. AND KETCHUP. SOOO MUCH KETCHUP. SHE'LL EAT PIZZA, BUT SHE RIPS THE CHEESE OFF FIRST."

SQUIR TTLL

EW.

14

MY DAD EATS CHEESE.

ON PIZZA?

HUH? OH, YEAH, WE ALL DO.

EXCEPT YOUR SISTER.

"MY DAD **REALLY** LIKES CHEESE. A LOT. A LOT-LOT."

IT'S WHAT'S FOR DINNER!

EXTRA SHARP

ANATOMY

of a "normal dinner" at our house

Milk or juice

Salad

Chips

Tacos

Guacamole (which we all actually like)

Baby carrots

Grated cheddar cheese

Taco Shells

TACO NIGHT? REAL WEIRD.

YEAH, BUT IT'S TACO NIGHT, LIKE, FOUR TIMES A WEEK.

HI, MOM! WHAT ARE WE...OH.

MOM? CAN YOU COME UP HERE?

WHAT IS IT, RAINA? YOU OKAY?

. . .

19

IS RAINA SICK, MOM?

YES. SHE NEEDS TO REST.

HEALTHY AS A HORSE!

COULD BE YOUR HORMONES KICKING IN . . . MIGHT HAVE BEEN A LITTLE FOOD POISONING.

COULD BE. BUT NONE OF THAT EXPLAINED WHY I HAD BEEN SO **SCARED.**

OKAY, CLASS, GETTING BACK TO THE QUIZ...

LATE

2. After dinner, 5/8 of the pizza is left over. That night, your sister eats 2/8 of the pizza. How much is left after that?

3. Henry spent 4/9 of his allowance on baseball cards. What fraction

IS THAT WITH OR WITHOUT THE CHEESE?

TABLE 3

THE NEXT DAY

RAINA, YOU ONLY ANSWERED TWO OUT OF EIGHT QUESTIONS.

IS EVERYTHING OKAY AT HOME?

shrug

ALL YOUR LITTLE DRAWINGS ARE VERY NICE . . . YOU'RE A VISUAL PROBLEM SOLVER.

BUT I STILL CAN'T GIVE YOU A GRADE HIGHER THAN A D-MINUS.

MY STOMACH HURTS.

29

AT LEAST IN THE SUMMER, WE COULD SPREAD THINGS OUT A LITTLE.

BZZZ

♪

YAWN

Bean Tacos

A LITTLE.

AMARAAAAA...

I'M HURRYING!

31

FIFTH GRADE (AND KINDERGARTEN FOR MY SISTER!) STARTED IN SEPTEMBER.

Itchy!

Dorky!

Fancy!

JANE AND NICOLE WERE IN MY CLASS AGAIN!

ROOM 2

MICHELLE, TOO.

MY TEACHER WAS MR. ABRAMS -- WHO I'D ACTUALLY HAD FOR SECOND GRADE, TOO.

HI, RAINA! GREAT TO SEE YOU AGAIN!

YEAH!

ONE OF THE THINGS OUR CLASS WOULD BE DOING THIS YEAR WAS THE

LDI!

THAT STANDS FOR

LECTURE, **D**EMONSTRATION, OR **I**NSTRUCTION!

ALMOST ANY SUBJECT IS FAIR GAME.

LECTURE
Tell us about something!
DEMONSTRATIO
Display a talent or skill!
INSTRUCTION
Lead us in creating something new!

LDIs WILL BE GIVEN ORALLY EVERY TUESDAY. YOU CAN SUBMIT PROPOSALS TO ME ANYTIME!

YES, TAI?

CAN I DEMONSTRATE HOW TO BURP THE ALPHABET?

Ha Ha Ha Ha Ha Ha

ORALLY.

OUT LOUD.

Chew

I HATE TALKING IN FRONT OF THE CLASS.

I GUESS I COULD DEMONSTRATE HOW I DRAW . . . BUT DRAWING IN FRONT OF PEOPLE IS **HARD.**

A FART CONTEST!

AND INSTRUCTION IS LIKE TEACHING. I CAN'T IMAGINE TEACHING **THESE** GUYS ANYTHING.

I WONDER IF IT'S TOO LATE TO TRANSFER TO A DIFFERENT CLASS?

ONE MORE THING!

GIRL SCOUTS!!

TODAY'S LDI
GIRL SCOUTS!
A lecture by
Jane + Raina

THE GIRL SCOUTS OF AMERICA WAS FOUNDED IN 1912 BY JULIETTE GORDON LOW IN SAVANNAH, GEORGIA.

THIS IS WHAT THE GIRL SCOUT LOGO LOOKS LIKE!

RAINA AND I ARE BOTH IN TROOP 415. I JOINED LAST YEAR...

SO FAR, SO GOOD.

WE DO ALL SORTS OF NEAT THINGS. CAMPING, VOLUNTEERING, COOKIE SALES...

AND THE BEST PART: EARNING BADGES!

RAINA'S GOING TO TELL YOU ALL ABOUT THEM!

...

gulp

THIS IS SO EMBARRASSING.

I ALMOST POOPED MY PANTS. WHAT AM I, A KINDERGA --

RAINA?

OH!! UM, JANE, IS THAT YOU??

Roll Roll Roll

YEAH, MR. ABRAMS SENT ME TO CHECK ON YOU. YOU OKAY?

FLUSH

YANK

I THINK SO . . .

NOW I'M SUPPOSED TO WALK YOU TO THE NURSE'S OFFICE.

A STOMACHACHE? I'M SORRY . . .

44

I'M FINE.

ARE YOU...

A POOPY DIAPER BABY??

NO!!!

IS THERE A PROBLEM, RAINA?

MICHELLE SAID I WAS... UM... SHE ASKED IF... I...

NEVER MIND.

JUST TRY AND BE A LITTLE KINDER TO MICHELLE, OKAY?

WHAT?!

SHE'S THE ONE WHO'S BEING MEAN!

I DON'T WANT TO HEAR ANY MORE.

BUT THAT'S NOT FAIR!

MOVING ON TO READING COMPREHENSION. PLEASE OPEN YOUR WORKBOOKS TO PAGE TWENTY-SIX . . .

48

LATER

DuckTales, WOO-OOO!

I'M HOME! WHO'S HUNGRY?

PIZZAAAAAAAAAAAAA!

(Cheeseless)

Shove

MR. ABRAMS'S NOTE SAID THAT JANE WILL GET AN A FOR THE LDI, BUT HE CAN ONLY GIVE YOU A B-MINUS BECAUSE YOU DIDN'T GIVE YOUR PORTION OF THE ORAL REPORT.

WHAT HAPPENED?

I JUST . . . GOT REALLY NERVOUS FOR SOME REASON!

I THOUGHT I WAS GONNA **PUKE!**

BUT . . . YOU DIDN'T!

NO . . . INSTEAD I JUST HAD TO GO TO THE BATHROOM REALLY BAD.

"NUMBER TWO."

I'LL TALK TO YOUR TEACHER, OKAY? FOR NOW JUST TRY AND GET SOME REST.

DON'T TELL HIM TOO MANY DETAILS.

I DON'T WANT EVERYONE TO THINK I'M A POOPY DIAPER BABY.

RINNNGGG

MAN, I'M HUNGRY.

Crinkle

Cold leftover artichoke

GAG!

MAN, I'M HUNGRY.

MAN, I HAVE NEVER BEEN SO HAPPY TO BE HOME...

OH YEAH...

YOU GO IN!

?

I'M GONNA... STAY OUT HERE FOR A BIT.

chew chew

HONEY, WHAT ARE WE GOING TO DO ABOUT THIS . . . PROBLEM?

I . . . I'M SORRY!! I DON'T WANT TO BE A PROBLEM.

WHAT IS IT YOU'RE SO **AFRAID** OF?

. . . VOMIT?

I WAS MISSING TOO MUCH SCHOOL.

I MADE YOU A HOT WATER BOTTLE.

BUT SCHOOL WAS THE LAST PLACE I WANTED TO BE.

CAN YOU BE SICK EVEN IF YOU'RE NOT **SICK?**

CAN YOU BE HEALTHY EVEN IF YOU HURT?

HI, RAINA. I'M LAUREN.

NOD

I'M GOING TO BE YOUR THERAPIST.

YOUR MOM AND DAD HAVE SPOKEN TO ME ABOUT WHAT'S BEEN GOING ON.

I'LL MEET WITH THEM OCCASIONALLY TO CHECK IN. BUT!

THIS IS ALL ABOUT **YOU.** I WANT TO MAKE SURE YOU FEEL COMFORTABLE HERE!

chew

THANK YOU, MRS. TELGEMEIER! SEE YOU IN A BIT.

GOOD LUCK!

CLICK!

THIS IS A SAFE SPACE, RAINA.

YOU CAN TALK ABOUT ANYTHING YOU LIKE.

SO . . . WILL YOU TELL ME A LITTLE ABOUT WHY YOU'RE HERE TODAY?

IN YOUR OWN WORDS?

UM . . .

Siblings

not enou space

School

fear of vomit

wond

SICKNESS

It's...

death

mean people

COMICS

Sleep

75

78

creeeeeakk

ALL DONE! I'LL SEE YOU NEXT WEEK, OKAY, RAINA?

'KAY.

SO?

IT SOUNDS LIKE YOU HAVE A LOT OF STRESSFUL THINGS GOING ON IN YOUR LIFE!

I GUESS SO.

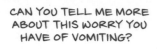
CAN YOU TELL ME MORE ABOUT THIS WORRY YOU HAVE OF VOMITING?

≥WHIMPER≥

DOES JUST HEARING THE WORD "VOMIT" SCARE YOU?

YES.

LET'S TALK ABOUT THAT AT YOUR NEXT SESSION!

SOUND GOOD?

YES...

...NO.

MR. ABRAMS?

I GOTTA GO -- IT'S AN EMERGENCY!

WHAT IF JANE'S THROWING UP?!!

OH NO . . . OH NO . . . I SAT NEXT TO HER ON THE BUS THIS MORNING . . .

OH NO, WE . . . WE SHARED SOME OF HER KIMBAP AT LUNCH TODAY . . .

SHE PROBABLY BREATHED ON ME . . .

AND OUR DESKS ARE NEXT TO EACH OTHER . . .

AND I'M SUPPOSED TO SLEEP OVER AT HER HOUSE THIS WEEKEND . . .

WHAT IF I'M NEXT?

WHAT IF

WHAT IF

WHAT IF . . .

WHAT?

UM . . . IS . . . ARE YOU OKAY?

YEAH . . .

OH, BECAUSE YOU RAN OUT OF CLASS SUPER FAST, AND --

I HAD TO GO TO THE BATHROOM.

YOU WERE GONE FOR LIKE FIFTEEN MINUTES!

SO?!

WHAT WERE YOU DOING IN THERE??

NONE OF YOUR BEESWAX, RAINA!

. . . DID YOU AT LEAST WASH YOUR HANDS?

89

ACTING "NORMAL" AT SCHOOL WAS GETTING HARDER AND HARDER.

OOH, CAN I HAVE A CHIP?

UM...

DID YOU WASH YOUR... I MEAN... ARE YOUR HANDS... UM...

YOU KNOW WHAT? JUST TAKE THE REST OF THEM. I'M NOT HUNGRY.

SWEET!

crunch crunch crunch

IF YOU'RE NOT GONNA EAT IT, I'LL GLADLY TAKE YOUR APPLE!

YEAH, CAN I HAVE YOUR JUICE BOX?

GREAT . . . NOW I'M WEIRD **AND** HUNGRY **AND** THIRSTY.

COFFEE . . . TEA . . . MILKSHAKE . . .

Pee

WHATEVER. WHO CARES IF MICHELLE SAYS THIS WATER FOUNTAIN IS PEE.

COFFEE . . . MOUNTAIN DEW . . . MILKSHAKE . . .

POO!!!

HA HA HA HA
HA HA HA HA
HA HA HA
HA

HA

I HATE YOUR GUTS, MICHELLE!!!

HA HA
HA

HA
HA

HA HA HA
HA

HA HA
HA

HI, RAINA. RECESS ISN'T OVER YET!

MICHELLE WAS BUGGING ME AGAIN.

I KNOW THE TWO OF YOU DON'T GET ALONG . . .

BUT IT'S POSSIBLE THAT YOU DON'T KNOW HER WHOLE STORY.

≥PFFT≤

A GREAT THINKER ONCE SAID: "BE KIND, FOR EVERYONE YOU MEET IS FIGHTING A HARD BATTLE."

IT DOESN'T DIMINISH YOUR **OWN** BATTLE . . .

BUT PERHAPS YOU AND MICHELLE CAN BECOME ALLIES INSTEAD OF ADVERSARIES.

chew

SATURDAY

You got it, dude.

DINNERTIME!

A TYPICAL DINNER AT JANE'S HOUSE LOOKS SOMETHING LIKE THIS!

Meat or fish

Rice

Tofu

Banchan (small dishes of food)

Soup

WHAT'S WRONG?

MY FAMILY DOESN'T REALLY COOK MEAT. I'M NOT USED TO . . . WELL . . . BONES.

HOW 'BOUT A DRIED SQUID TENTACLE? THESE ARE **SO** GOOD.

NO . . . THAT'S OKAY.

YOUR LOSS.

I DO LIKE CABBAGE...

place

munch

YUM!

I'LL HAVE SOME MORE OF THAT, TOO!!

NEXT MORNING

WAKE UP! I'M STARVING! YOU WANT FRENCH TOAST?

I'M NOT THAT HUNGRY. I WAS A LITTLE... GASSY ALL NIGHT.

DOES KIMCHI CAUSE GAS?

I **NEVER** HAVE GAS.

THAT NIGHT WE WENT TO SIZZLER, WHICH HAS AN AWESOME ALL-YOU-CAN-EAT SALAD BAR.

OH, WAIT... BEANS GIVE YOU GAS.

CHEESE... THAT MIGHT BE BAD.

POTATO SALAD... I'VE HEARD THAT CAN HAVE BACTERIA IN IT.

CABBAGE... NO...

...

PIZZA.

PIZZA DOESN'T MAKE YOU SICK?

NO, BUT IT MAKES **AMARA** SICK! THAT'S WHY SHE DOESN'T EAT THE CHEESE. ONE TIME, WHEN SHE WAS THREE, WE WERE AT OUR NEIGHBORS' HOUSE, AND SHE WAS EATING SOME PIZZA, AND SHE CHOKED, AND --

OKAY.

SO PIZZA DOESN'T MAKE YOU SICK. WHAT ELSE?

...

OH! BURGER KING HAMBURGERS!

BUT MY **MOM** WON'T EAT MEAT! SHE HATES IT! DO YOU WANT TO KNOW WHY?! ONE TIME, WHEN I WAS A BABY, SHE HAD THIS CRAZY DREAM WHERE --

RAINA, YOU SEEM VERY PREOCCUPIED WITH THE THINGS OTHER PEOPLE EAT.

WHY?

...I DUNNO.

YOU REALIZE THAT YOU ONLY HAVE CONTROL OVER YOURSELF, RIGHT?

THERE ARE **MANY** THINGS YOU SIMPLY HAVE NO CONTROL OVER!

YEAH... NO JOKE!!

LAUREN EXPLAINED THAT FEARS OFTEN HAVE NO RHYME OR REASON...

BUT THAT WE ALL HAVE SOME LEVEL OF SELF-CONTROL.

pluck

SO MAYBE...

:chew:

I COULD LEARN TO HAVE CONTROL OVER MY FEARS, TOO.

SWALLOW

SHORTLY THEREAFTER I DISCOVERED:

MARINATED ARTICHOKE HEARTS ARE GOOD ON SALAD.

- Lettuce
- Croutons
- Italian dressing
- Artichokes!

AND ON PIZZA!

MMM.

EVEN STRAIGHT FROM THE JAR!

SO I'M NOT AFRAID OF EATING ARTICHOKES ANYMORE! ISN'T THAT COOL? DOES THAT MEAN **I'M CURED??**

SOMETIMES WE HAVE THINGS IN LIFE WE NEED TO WORK ON.

BUT THAT DOESN'T MEAN WE'RE SICK.

IT'S NOT AS SIMPLE AS HAVING A PHYSICAL ILLNESS, OR A CURE.

OH.

BUT I'M GLAD YOU'RE EATING ARTICHOKES AGAIN!

FOOD FOR THOUGHT!

HOW COME YOU'RE LATE FOR SCHOOL SO MUCH?

UM . . .

BECAUSE I GO TO A THERAPIST.

113

LAST YEAR, BODILY FUNCTIONS WERE COMMON CURRENCY.

THIS YEAR...

IS THE DOOR STUCK?

EVERYTHING WAS PRIVATE.

?

Shhhhhh

whisper
giggle

A MYSTERY.

BAM

Ha Ha Ha Ha
Ha!   Ha

THE BOYS HADN'T GOTTEN THE MEMO YET.

Today's LDI:
The Anatomy
of a FART!!
by Tai!

BUT IT SEEMED LIKE THE GIRLS WERE SLOWLY FORMING A SECRET CLUB...

TO WHICH I WAS NOT INVITED.

SHRUG

117

LATER

EVERYONE'S ACTING WEIRD, HUH? I GUESS YOU'RE ALL AT **THAT AGE.**

WHAT AGE?

TEN?

PUBERTY.

OHHHH.

EWWWW.

120

OKAY, OKAY . . . A YOUNG PERSON. A **MINOR.**

BETTER.

SO, IS SOMETHING WRONG WITH ME?

LAUREN JUST THINKS YOU COULD USE A LITTLE MORE SPACE.

rustle

YOU'VE SHARED A BEDROOM SINCE AMARA WAS BORN!

SO, WHAT -- ARE ALL FOUR OF **YOU** GOING TO SHARE A ROOM? WE ONLY HAVE TWO OF THEM . . .

LISTEN, IF YOU'D RATHER WE GIVE THIS SPACE TO YOUR SISTER OR BROTHER...

NO NO NO NO...

SHOOOOF

THAT NIGHT

HUH.

NO MORE BUNK BED...

NO ONE WATCHING ME...

cuddle snuggle

SNORE

NO SOUND BARRIER!!!

crunch

MORNING, KIDDO. SLEEP OKAY?

NOOOOOOOOOO

HOW DO YOU PUT UP WITH DAD'S SNORING?!

I GUESS I JUST GOT USED TO IT!

MAYBE I COULD, LIKE, SLEEP DOWN HERE ON THE COUCH OR SOMETHING?

NOPE. YOUR GRANDMA'S COMING TO LIVE WITH US FOR A LITTLE WHILE.

WHAAA?

WHERE CAN I PUT MY SHOES?

JUST THROW THEM ON TOP OF THE PILE.

MY SISTERS AND I WERE LUCKY TO EVEN **HAVE** SHOES! WE LIVED THREE MILES OUTSIDE OF PINCKNEYVILLE, AND EVERY DAY WE'D WALK TO . . .

LET'S GO TO **MY** ROOM!

WANNA SEE THE COMICS I'VE BEEN MAKING?

SHOOOOF

HA HA!

OH MY GOSH . . .

IS THAT YOUR DAD?!

THE SNORING ONE?

YEAH!

THESE ARE SO COOL! HOW DO YOU **DO** THIS?!

I JUST KINDA LOOK AROUND ME, AND LISTEN TO WHAT PEOPLE SAY . . .

THEN I MAKE COMICS ABOUT IT!

I WISH I COULD DRAW.

TRY!

NO . . . I'VE TRIED. I CAN'T.

I'VE SEEN YOU DRAW PRECIOUS KITTY . . . C'MON!

NO . . . I . . . I JUST TRACE HER.

THAT'S OKAY.

HOWL!!!

click.

WHIIIINE

SORRY WILL'S SO FUSSY, EVERYONE...

THAT'S OKAY. THIS IS GOOD SOURCE MATERIAL!

YOWL!

Hee!

THE NEXT DAY

BIG GAME TODAY!! EVERYONE EXCITED?

ZZZ

I'M GOING UPSTAIRS.

AWW, C'MON!

RAINA! RAINA?

SHOOooF

RAINA!

POP!

?

HELLO?

JANE? IS THAT YOU? WHAT'S WRONG? I CAN'T UNDERSTAND YOU . . .

WE'RE **MOVING.**

YOU ARE? WHERE?

THE SUBURBS. OVER NEAR THE AIRPORT.

WHEN?

UMMA AND APPA SAID WE CAN FINISH OUT THE SCHOOL YEAR HERE... BUT THEN WE'RE GOING AWAY. I WON'T KNOW **ANYBODY** IN MY NEW TOWN.

MY DENTIST IS NEAR THE AIRPORT. IT'S NOT **THAT** FAR.

AND DO YOU REMEMBER ROSA FROM THIRD GRADE?

HER FAMILY LIVES OVER THERE NOW, TOO.

HOOONK!

THEY HAVE A BIG HOUSE WITH FOUR BEDROOMS AND A TREE HOUSE AND A CREEK IN THEIR BACKYARD! AND A **GAZEBO**!!

I BET YOU AND YOUR BROTHER WILL EACH GET YOUR OWN ROOM! SO LUCKY! IT'S SO NICE AND SUNNY BY THE AIRPORT! I'D **LOVE** IT IF MY FAMILY --

RAINA!!!

I DON'T WANT TO GO.

OKAY?

138

MICHELLE'S TURN TO GIVE AN LDI CAME AROUND.

TODAY'S LDI:
Healthy Food w/ Michelle!

I'M GOING TO DEMONSTRATE HOW TO MAKE WALDORF SALAD!

IT'S ONE OF MY FAMILY'S FAVORITE DISHES.

THE INGREDIENTS ARE APPLES, CELERY, WALNUTS . . .

THAT SOUNDS OKAY!

AND **MAYONNAISE!**

EW!!!

MICHELLE, PLEASE CONTINUE.

RAINA, CAN I SEE YOU IN THE HALL?

SO FIRST YOU CHOP THE APPLE INTO BITE-SIZED PIECES...

I'M SORRY . . . IT'S JUST . . . APPLES AND **MAYONNAISE?!!**

GAG!

I THINK THAT SOUNDS DELICIOUS!

MR. BRAMS
FIFTH GRADERS

EVERYONE EATS DIFFERENT THINGS. WE ALL HAVE OUR LIKES AND DISLIKES.

BUT PLEASE, **PLEASE** TRY NOT TO BE DISRESPECTFUL OF OTHER PEOPLE.

TREAT OTHERS AS YOU WISH TO BE TREATED.

SO, IN NON-TEACHER-SPEAK, I THINK THAT MEANS . . .

144

145

SO WHAT IS **YOUR** DEAL?

YOU GIVE AWAY YOUR LUNCHES, YOU DIDN'T WANT MICHELLE'S SALAD . . .

DO YOU HAVE AN **EATING DISORDER??!**

NO!

NAH, SHE'S JUST A WEIRDO.

DINA!!

SEE? YOU WON'T HAVE TO GO TO MIDDLE SCHOOL WITH ANY OF **THESE** MEANIES.

YOU GET A FRESH START!

I DON'T WANT A FRESH START.

THE IDEA OF LEAVING MAKES ME WANT TO PUKE.

THE IDEA OF **PUKING** MAKES ME WANT TO . . .

NEVER EAT RUN HIDE SCREAM NOT TOUCH THINGS

147

PROBABLY LIKE . . . A FIVE.

IT MAKES MY STOMACH HURT.

AND THEN I GET SCARED I'M GOING TO PUKE.

AND **THAT** MAKES ME FEEL . . . ABOUT AN EIGHT OR A NINE.

AS FAR AS BEING SCARED GOES.

I DON'T WANT THEM TO KNOW THAT I'M AFRAID OF THROW-UP.

IT'S JUST SO...

BABYISH.

WEIRD.

DUMB.

STUPID.

I BET ALL YOUR FRIENDS ARE SECRETLY SCARED OF SOMETHING!

LET'S GO BACK TO BREATHING. JUST... BREATHE.

FEET.

GROUND.

BREATHE.

LAUREN SAYS YOU'RE MAKING **JOKES!**

WHICH IS A SIGN OF **PROGRESS!**

THEY SAY LAUGHTER IS THE BEST MEDICINE.

WANT TO READ THIS COMIC STRIP JANE AND I MADE?

Hm.

VERY NICE.

YOU GONNA SHOW JANE TOMORROW?

YEAH, AFTER THERAPY!

DO **YOU** THINK THIS IS FUNNY, GRANDMA?

I'LL TELL YOU WHAT'S FUNNY! MY BROTHER LOUIE HAD A DOG -- A MUTT, REAL MANGY. THE DOG HATED SQUIRRELS. ONE DAY . . .

THE NEXT DAY

slam

THIS ISN'T FUNNY!!!

JANE, WHAT'S GOING ON?

YOU WEREN'T ON THE BUS THIS MORNING, SO MICHELLE SAT WITH ME INSTEAD.

SHE'S ACTUALLY REALLY NICE ONCE YOU GET TO KNOW HER!

BUT I WON'T LET HER COME BETWEEN US.

PROMISE!

MORNING, HONEY. TIME TO GET UP FOR SCHOOL!

CAN I STAY HOME? MY STOMACH HURTS.

YEP... STILL HEALTHY AS A HORSE.

NO PARASITES, NO BACTERIA, NO FOOD ALLERGIES . . .

UM, GOOD?

SO YOUR OFFICIAL DIAGNOSIS IS **IBS.**

THAT STANDS FOR **IRRITABLE BOWEL SYNDROME.**

IT BASICALLY MEANS UPSET STOMACH . . . WITH NO DISCERNABLE CAUSE.

TAKAHASHI

CAN IT BE CURED?

IT TENDS TO COME AND GO.

GET ENOUGH REST, EXERCISE, WATER . . .

THESE ARE MY LAST FEW WEEKS OF LIVING HERE.

I WANT THEM TO BE **GOOD** ONES.

MR. ABRAMS!! I GOTTA --

GO AHEAD, MICHELLE.

I JUST DON'T GET IT.

SHE'S BEEN MEAN TO US FOR **YEARS.**

I KNOW . . .

I THINK SHE HAD A CHANGE OF HEART.

WHAT IF IT'S A TRICK?

WHAT IF SHE JUST NEEDS FRIENDS?

YOU DON'T HAVE TO BE BEST FRIENDS WITH HER, BUT TRY AND ACCEPT THAT SHE'S **MY** FRIEND NOW.

PLEASE?

AND WHO KNOWS. MAYBE PUBERTY MADE HER NICE!

CAN PUBERTY MAKE YOU **NICE?!**

HA! I DON'T KNOW IF IT CAN BE SCIENTIFICALLY PROVEN...

BUT WE ALL GO THROUGH CHANGES AND TIMES OF REFLECTION.

GROWTH IS BOTH PHYSICAL AND EMOTIONAL, YOU KNOW!

HOW ARE YOU FEELING ABOUT EVERYTHING IN YOUR LIFE LATELY?

Earplugs

Z

SNORE

I CAN TRY.

NOW, YOU DON'T HAVE TO ANSWER . . .

BUT I WANT YOU ALL TO THINK ABOUT SOMETHING THAT SCARES YOU.

AND NOW . . . TRY AND NOTICE HOW THAT MAKES YOU **FEEL**.

FOR ME . . . WORRYING ABOUT THINGS MAKES MY STOMACH HURT.

AND MY STOMACH HURTING . . . MAKES ME WORRY MORE.

IT'S A CYCLE.

MIND AND BODY.

BODY AND MIND.

BUT, I HAVE A FEW WAYS OF COPING.

CAN EVERYONE PLEASE STAND?

I SHOWED THEM HOW TO BREATHE DEEPLY.

AND HOW TO FOCUS ON THEIR FEET.

AMAZINGLY, I GOT THROUGH MY PRESENTATION WITHOUT A HINT OF FEAR.

CLAP CLAP CLAP CLAP CLAP CLAP CLAP CLAP

AND **EVERYONE** SEEMED A LITTLE CALMER AFTERWARD.

OR MAYBE
NOT.

HER FAMILY HAS ASKED ME NOT TO SHARE MORE THAN THAT.

AWWW!!!

IS IT A SECRET?

NOT REALLY.

JUST CONFIDENTIAL, OUT OF RESPECT FOR MICHELLE'S PRIVACY.

YES, NICOLE?

WAS IT SOMETHING CONTAGIOUS?!?

NOPE! IT'S NOT SOMETHING YOU CAN CATCH.

WHEW!

THE GOOD NEWS IS, SHE'S GOING TO BE FINE.

THE BAD NEWS IS...

MR. ABRAMS?

YES, RAINA?

I HAVE AN IDEA.

cheese & artichokes!

WHAT SHOULD WE DO NOW?

I DUNNO, WHAT DO **YOU** GUYS WANNA DO?

WE COULD PLAY SKELETONS IN THE CLOSET...

WHAT'S THAT?

IT'S WHERE EVERYONE TELLS THEIR DEEPEST...

DARKEST...

SECRET.

I'M NOT SO SURE I LIKE THIS GAME...

I'LL START. I...I...

I GOT MY PERIOD!!

WHAT?!

WHEN?

STARTING IN MARCH!

WOWWWWW.

IS THAT REALLY A DEEP AND DARK SECRET?

THE WAY EVERYONE **ACTS** ABOUT IT? **YEAH.**

I GUESS.

MY BIG SISTER GOT HERS A FEW YEARS AGO, SO I KIND OF KNEW WHAT TO EXPECT.

BUT IT'S STILL SUPER WEIRD.

...

So cool

So mature

REALLY?!

YEAH. IT'S NO BIG DEAL.

BUT NO ONE **EVER** TALKS ABOUT IT!

I ACTUALLY THOUGHT THAT MAYBE . . .

THERE WAS SOMETHING REALLY WRONG WITH ME.

YOUR TURN, RAINA!!

BUT . . . I HAVE NO IDEA WHAT TO SAY!

TRY.

Breeeathe

HI, MICHELLE?

HI.

I'M . . . I'M GLAD YOU'RE OKAY.

THIS WAS MY THIRD INTESTINAL SURGERY! THE FIRST TWO WERE WHEN I WAS A BABY.

WOW. I HAD NO IDEA!

WERE YOU SCARED?

YEAH, BUT LIKE . . .

I NEEDED TO TAKE THE RISK.

DID YOU . . . UM . . .

DID YOU THROW UP?!

NO! BUT BEFORE MY SURGERY I WAS SO NERVOUS I **THOUGHT** I MIGHT PUKE!

BUT GUESS WHAT?

WHAT?

YOU KNOW THAT BREATHING THING YOU SHOWED US IN CLASS?

I TRIED IT.

AND IT HELPED A LOT.

THANK YOU.

. . . YOU'RE WELCOME!

SO . . . DID YOU GET THE POSTER WE MADE YOU?

HECK YEAH, I DID!!

208

OH . . . I GUESS I SHOULD GO.

HEY, MICHELLE?

YOU'VE GOT GUTS.

HA! WELL, THANKS.

SEE YA IN MIDDLE SCHOOL?

YEAH.

MY MOM SAID SHE'LL DRIVE ME TO YOUR NEW HOUSE ANYTIME I WANT.

MAYBE WE CAN STILL WRITE AND DRAW TOGETHER!

SURE!

AND GO ON BIKE RIDES!

AND TO THE MALL!

AND SEE MOVIES! AND GO FOR PIZZA! EAT KOREAN FOOD! GIRL SCOUT CAMP! ROLLER-SKATING! BIRTHDAY PARTIES!

Z

THE END

Thanks to . . .

Early readers: Andy Runton, Vera Brosgol, Casey Gilly, Mike Jung, Shannon Hale, and Sue Telgemeier.

Consultants: Dr. Judy Pelham and Dr. Frank F. Escobar-Roger.

Production assistant: Meggie Ramm.

The team at Scholastic: Cassandra Pelham Fulton, David Saylor, Phil Falco, Lauren Donovan, Ellie Berger, Tracy van Straaten, Lizette Serrano, Julie Amitie, Carmen Alvarez, Susan Lee, Holland Baker, Celia Lee, Akshaya Iyer, and Shivana Sookdeo.

Colorists: Braden Lamb and Shelli Paroline.

My agent, Judy Hansen.

My family!

My therapists!!

My lovely and comforting group of friends, for whom no topic is off-limits.

My readers, who always ask the best questions.

—Raina

Author's Note

Guts was inspired by real people, real therapy, and real memories from my fourth- and fifth-grade years, though I adjusted some minor details to make the reading experience more streamlined.

I've dealt with stomachaches and anxiety for most of my life. It has never been easy, but it's gotten better as I've learned how to manage it over the years. My panic attacks came out of nowhere, starting at age nine. I missed a lot of school. I became obsessed with every little funny feeling in my stomach. I was terrified of eating the "wrong" foods, convinced they would make me ill. (The clinical term for fear of vomit is *emetophobia*, and it's actually pretty common!)

So, how am I doing now, more than three decades after this story takes place?

In the past five years I have done talk therapy, cognitive behavioral therapy, mindfulness training, EMDR, and exposure therapy. I tried anxiety medication. I use meditation apps. They've all helped, but I've realized that my phobias and worries are just part of who I am. I do my best to manage them!

I've been tested for everything from celiac disease to Crohn's disease to ulcerative colitis, and, after many negative results, I've learned to accept that there's nothing medically "wrong" with my stomach. I just have a sensitive system and must be careful about what I eat. My anxiety also affects how my body feels! So when I'm stressed out, I'm more likely to have digestion issues.

I want to make sure my readers know that this is my personal story. You may recognize some of my struggles, or yours might be totally different. You might not experience physical or emotional stress at all. If you do find yourself feeling stressed, or you're hurting in a way that you don't understand, please talk to an adult you know and trust. I was very lucky to have people in my life who supported me and helped me find ways to feel better.

Finally, I want to encourage you to talk about how you feel. You can write it down, draw pictures or comics, make music or plays, or simply share with your friends. It takes guts to admit how you feel on the inside, but chances are, others will be able to relate. You won't know unless you try!

Also by
Raina Telgemeier

Smile

Sisters

By Ann M. Martin
and Raina Telgemeier